SECRETS OF OFFLINE MARKETING PROFITS

How To Wake Up The Marketing Genius Inside of You

JUAN MARCIAL

Lulu Publishing Services rev. date: 10/25/2019

This Book Will Show You How To Put Creative Marketing, Free Publicity, and Strategic Joint Ventures to Work for <u>Your</u> Business So You Can Sit Back And Watch Your Profits Explode!

ABOUT THE AUTHOR

**Juan Marcial The King Of Marketing And Promotions
Founder of the Profit Potentials Network Inc.**

Juan Marcial has been an Enterpreneur for many many years since a young age.He is also a Real Estate Investor and own properties in Florida, Pennsylvania, Mississippi, Missouri, Tennessee, Texas, Arizona and Puerto Rico. He actually Failed in the past in many businesses until he discovered the Secrets of why so many businesses failed while they "apparently" were trying to do everything possible to succeed. He actually Discovered that the Main Cause of Failure specially on Small and Medium size businesses is Poor Marketing Practices. He then dedicated a great part of his life (and a Great deal of Money) to learn and became an Expert on Marketing, Copywriting, Advertising, Sales and Promotions with Great Success in many business areas and is acually a Consultant for Small and Medium Size businesses. He is also a Member of The American Writers and Artists (AWAI) and has also been a Rosicrucian all his life. He has Studied the work of Dan Kennedy, Jay Abraham, John Carlton, Gary Halbert, Brendon Burchard, Dan Lok and T. Harv Eker whom he Consider his Mentors...

In Memory of Dan Kennedy

From Whom I Learned So Many Wonderful Things

About Marketing, Copywriting, Sales and Ethics in Business

I want to Dedicate This Book

Contents

Introduction: John Ritskowitz hosted a teleseminar with Michel Fortin, David Garfinkel, Yanik Silver, and JP Maroney. Entitled "Million Dollar Roundtable," it was a chance for these marketing pros to share some of their best secrets for marketing offline, which is something more online Marketers should be doing. Ideally we should all be marketing both offline and online.

Well these folks delivered the goods, and while the call lasted about 2 hours, it still wasn't enough time to get to everything (it never is, right?). So John compiled some of the ideas they talked about on the call, plus lots more ideas to cover the offline marketing spectrum.

Some of these ideas are more traditional, such as yellow pages advertising and classified ads. Of course that doesn't mean they should be neglected.

Other ideas are traditional, but not used as much, or I should say not always used as effectively as they could. Direct response marketing and publicity are two that come to mind.

And then there are really creative ideas that are often overlooked, such as valuable joint ventures and strategic alliances. **Some of these ideas have the potential to really deliver a lot of leads and sales with minimal traditional "work."**

One thing we highly recommend right now: Please read this book out, with pen and highlighter in hand. Otherwise, we all know how many books we have sitting on our Shelves, never to be read or acted upon. Don't let that happen here.**There are too many great ideas here not to take action.**

You'll find these ideas start out somewhat simplistically and gradually get more creative and complex. So dig in and start thinking about how you could apply these ideas to your business today!

Part I - Traditional Offline Marketing

Don't think of these methods as too simple or mundane. They are very effective when done right and combined with other techniques in this book.

- 📂① **Classified Ads** – This is something everyone should be testing in some form or another. It's great for lead generations. You should still have a strong benefit-driven headline and a clear call to action. Free reports work very well with classifieds. My local paper, the Hartford Courant even has an ongoing deal of 3 lines for 3 days – for free! Even adding more lines only ends up costing a few bucks. With a price like that, there's no reason anyone with a website should not be testing ways to draw traffic to the site with classifieds.

- 📄① **Direct Mail** – Nothing beats direct response when it comes to results-driven proven advertising. And messages sent directly to your highly targeted market via direct mail can deliver a terrific return on investment (ROI) when tested properly. There's a wealth of information on direct marketing by Michel Fortin, David Garfinkel, Gary Halbert, Dan Kennedy, and many more experts. Here are some sites where you can learn more:

  - ❖ http://www.thegaryhalbertletter.com - Home of the Gary Halbert Letter
  - ❖ http://www.dankennedy.com - Dan Kennedy's site
  - ❖ http://www.srds.com - The Standard Rate & Data (SRDS) List Book, a great resource to locate mailing lists of nearly any type you can imagine. You can also find it in some larger city libraries.
  - ❖ http://www.referenceusa.com - Reference USA is a great place to get compiled lists by industry, SIC, demographics and more. It contains names, addresses

and lots of other great information on more than 12 million U.S. businesses, 102 million U.S. residents, 683,000 U.S. health care providers, 1 million Canadian businesses, and 11 million Canadian residents.

❖ http://www.usps.com - The US Postal Service website has a variety of tools and educational materials about direct mail as well.

📄① **Postcards** – Yes, postcards are a form of direct mail, but it warrants its own category. Postcards are cheaper to produce and mail than full-blown direct mail packages or sales letters, and they are great for generating leads. Like classified ads, a free report or free gift often works well here. Postcards are also a great way to stay in touch with your customers and prospects, and they also work well as part of a sequence of mailings. A good place to go for customized postcards is http://www.usps.com (the US Postal Service website), because the USPS has partnered with a company that will print and mail your postcards for you! Best of all, you only pay for the postage (i.e. FREE printing costs). **Hint:** be sure to include yourself on the mailing list so you can get your own mailing as well.

📄① **Yellow Pages** – Another great resource that is often underutilized or used ineffectively. Yellow page ads are great because when someone sees your ad, they are already in the market for your product or service. Yellow page ads need to be benefits-driven, with your Unique Selling Proposition (USP) stated clearly and boldly (remember, this is the one place where your prospects will see your ad alongside all of your competitors). You want your ad to stand out from the clutter. Use a direct response type of ad, and again, free gifts or premiums work well here.

Gary Halbert has written about yellow pages several times in his newsletter. To find them easily, just enter the following search at Google:

site:thegaryhalbertletter.com +"yellow page"

Another great resource that JP Maroney recommends is Alan Saltz's course on the subject, available at http://www.yellowpagesprofit.com

Space Ads – If you're going to do a space ad, it will generally get better results if you use the same layout as the editorials. Use the same font styles and sizes for the headline, body, etc. If the newspaper uses 2 columns per article on the page your ad will appear, use 2 columns in your ad. If they use 3 columns, you use 3. The "advertorial" approach almost always does better than traditional space ads that scream "ad."

A great way to get very low costs space ads is to use what's known as remnant, or standby advertising. Enter the following search in Google to see what I mean and to learn more:

site:thegaryhalbertletter.com +"Nancy Jones"

And you'll learn to experiment in many creative ways to find out what works for you. A local advertising paper, the *Rare Reminder* here in the Hartford area, has classified ads and space ads. But I noticed that one "stone and mulch" company has their space ad featured upside-down in every weekly issue. At first I thought it was a mistake. But after seeing it upside-down week after week, I suspected they found that their upside-down ad stands out from the clutter. People think it's a mistake and read it. Yes, it's a gimmick. Would I do it? Only if it tested positively. And maybe it has for these folks. Food for thought.

⧗① **Radio/TV/Infomercials** – You might be surprised how inexpensive you can get these types of slots, especially if you use remnant advertising. Study the best infomercials, for example (the ones you see over and over again...they must be working or they wouldn't keep airing them), to get some ideas on how they are constructed.

▦① **Flyers** – Who says you can't hire a high school student to stuff mailboxes or stick 'em under windshields? Obviously if you are selling a high-priced financial course, it would be better to target the windshields of a fancy hotel than your local Wal-Mart. And I believe the US Postal Service also prints them for you like they do postcards if you want to mail them. Check out http://www.usps.com

⌐①① **Networking** – Your local Chamber of Commerce, trade shows, seminars, and anywhere your prospects hang out are all good opportunities for networking. In many cases, the hotel bar the night before the seminar is the best opportunity for making contacts. It's usually more effective to try to capture contacts and leads than to try to close a sale on the spot, so get your elevator speech ready and have plenty of business cards on hand.

☎① **Telemarketing** – Remember the "Do Not Call" list only applies to consumers, so if you do any kind of business to business selling, telemarketing is a viable marketing method you can use effectively. Also, the "Do Not Call" list may not apply to you with your customers or if you already have a relationship with your prospects.

🗀⊐① **A Trade Show Booth** – A great place to capture leads. Again, a free report or gift does wonders. When you get a long line waiting at your booth, many people will stop by just to see what the fuss is about. Make your sales materials and sales people benefit-driven. Remember what your prospects are thinking: "What's in it for me?"

⌲⌲① **Blimps, Banners, and Billboards** – If it's zoned for advertising and it's blank, you have an opportunity.

⌲▤① **Door Hangers** – Those same high school students can help you with door hangers as well.

⌲▤① **Circulars** – Again, high school students can also help you hand out circulars, post them on community bulletin boards, on telephone poles, wherever. You can make a donation to your local church and ask them if you can leave a stack at their next bake sale or bingo event. And certainly you can arrange to have your circular included in your local newspaper or community paper. For your money, circulars are very inexpensive to print and distribute.

⌲▤① **Card Decks** – These stacks of index cards are mailed to targeted audiences. Each deck can contain anywhere from 50 to 200 cards or so, each with an advertisement or coupon. They may also double as a business reply card on back. Since your ad is mixed in with tons of others, it's especially important to have a great headline and layout that will stand out from the clutter.

Card decks are inexpensive because all of the advertisers are sharing the cost of the mailing. They can cost as little as three cents a prospect for large mailings. Even for smaller mailings, they are generally cheap, which is good for testing.

Make sure you choose your audience wisely. Card decks are great for targeting a niche. Free reports or books work especially well here, because the person flipping through the cards will be attracted to the word "FREE." As always, make sure there is a clear call to action. Multiple methods of response usually work better than a single method. For example, they can drop the card in the mail, call a free recorded message, go to your website, etc. And you may have some options with remnant space, so always try to negotiate a lower price (how hard is it for them to stick another card in their mailing...their costs are incremental and their profit is high even on remnant rates).

A couple other tips: When you see repeat advertisers in a deck, you have a pretty good idea that the deck is working for that ad. If that ad also targets your niche market, it may be a good one to test in. Also, test with copy that you already know works.

📁✦ **Value-Paks** – Similar to card decks, "value-paks" are little booklets with multiple ads. They are mostly used with coupons, rather than business reply cards.

📁✦ **Ad Magazines** – You've seen them. Magazines that are little more than a collection of space ads. They are usually local, and the ads in them usually aren't direct response. By putting your direct response ad there, you stand out over all the other ads. But the downside is that these magazines tend to be less niche-focused (although there are certainly exceptions, with the real estate and automobile-themed magazines and newspapers).

📁✦ **Catalogues** – Your catalog doesn't have to look like L.L. Bean or the like to be effective. A good one to study with respect to the ads themselves is the J. Peterman catalogue (check out http://www.jpeterman.com).

Here's a good way to start small and work up from there in developing a good catalogue:

a) Try a simple double-sided flyer first and test response.

b) Make sure you locate highly targeted lists, as the wasted cost of mailings is going to be your biggest expense.
c) Continue to expand, test, and tweak. Test everything—your layout, your copy, your prices—until you find the best combination.

Part II - Creative Offline Marketing

📁✏️① **Package Inserts** – If you're going to mail out a product or package to a customer anyway, always tuck a sales letter for another product in the package. It won't cost you any more, and when your customer receives that package, he or she will be pleased with the product (assuming your product isn't junk) and be more favorable towards another purchase from you. You can also joint venture with other companies that target your niche market and get them to include your insert when shipping their product.

📁✏️① **Mini-seminars** – A great way to bundle up all of your products and services and sell them from the platform. It's very inexpensive to rent a hall and put on a 2 hour presentation for your target market on something that interests them. You position yourself as the expert, and you get to pitch your products and services. Be sure to record the event and offer it to other prospects who may not be able to attend the presentation in person.

Speakers don't get paid, but still make money by pitching their products. It works, and anyone who doesn't have one or more of these planned is missing out of a lot of extra potential income.

📄📁① **Teleseminars** – Basically a conference call, we've all probably been on many of them. Some have organized them and have been speakers. They can be pure content (i.e. no obvious pitches) for strengthening social proof and building up anticipation for a new product to be released in the future. They can be a mixture of content and pitch. You can even arrange a series of them as a tele-course and charge big money to attend (Marc Goldman and Jay Abraham did this with a six-month long series, one per month, on joint ventures and deal making).

Voice Broadcasts – A very under-utilized technique. If you have an existing relationship with your customers or prospects, the Do Not Call list does not apply. That sets the stage for a great way to call thousands of your customers simultaneously when they are most likely to be away from home. You simply upload your customer's phone numbers, record the message you want to leave, and the technology does the rest.

Example: "Hi, this is John Smith. Sorry I missed you, but I wanted to let you know that our firesale is ending tomorrow…"

Voice broadcasts work best when they are part of a sequence.

Example: "Hi, this is John Smith calling, from Smith Publishing. I'm sorry that I missed you, but I wanted to let you know about a valuable letter and free gift we're sending to your home. You should be getting it in the next day or two. Just look for the bright blue envelope…"

Gift Certificates – It's generally known that people will usually spend more than the gift certificate amount. So if you operate a jewelry store, and you mail your customers a free no-obligation $25 gift certificate, it's usually a very sound investment. Most restaurant owners already know that people generally don't dine alone, so by giving your customers a free gift certificate, they're bound to bring in others who will spend more money on food and drinks. A good variation on this formula is the free birthday dinner. Generally, nobody is going to come in on their birthday and eat their free dinner by themselves. They're going to bring friends, relatives, you get the idea.

Here's a great way to use gift certificates to get referrals: Send a letter to your customers with three gift certificates.

One they can use for themselves, and the other two they can give away to friends or relatives. They keep your customers happy (and happy customers are more likely to speak highly of you to others) and they compound that fact by letting your customers give the certificates to others, to whom they will sing your praises. It's like a tell-a-friend script on steroids!

📄📄① **Coupons** – Like gift certificates, coupons are also a great way to "touch" your customers and bring them back into your store (or website or whatever).

📄📄① **Contests** – The sandwich chain Subway recently had a scratch-off contest, but you had to go online to see if you were a winner. Contests are a great way to get leads and generate sales. **Here's a tip:** always include an unadvertised "second place" that everyone who didn't win will get. Joe Vitale did that last year, and used an email and voice broadcast to announce your "second place" prize. I would have included a sequence of direct mail as well, but the premise is the same.

Also, the Nathan's hot dog eating contest is a great example of using their product in the contest itself. If your product or service lends itself well to this approach, consider testing it.

📄📄① **Celebrity Endorsements** – They aren't as expensive as you might think (unless you try to get Sean Connery or Tom Cruise). The key is that you need to use celebrities that your target market recognizes as such. So Tony Rice would make a great celebrity for bluegrass and acoustic guitar enthusiasts. Not so much for gardening fans.

📄📄① **CD Salesletter** – People generally won't read 90 minutes worth of copy, but they will listen to it. The perceived value is much higher than a traditional salesletter as well. They can listen to it in their cars, on their walkmans (although today everyone has an iPod...why not use a podcast instead?). The point is that you can cram in a lot more information. You can do testimonials in their own voices, have sound effects or music. Anything to help advance the sale.

Thank You Letters – Whether you send gift certificates, coupons, a 2 for 1 special, a free gift, or just a friendly thank you letter to stay on your customer's radar screen, these types of letters are memorable and encourage your customers to send you referrals. As always, these types of letters should be personalized, and *never* use a mailing address letter on the envelope.

Example:

Dear Mr. Smith,

I hope you are very pleased with your recent purchase of my quality artwork. May it bring much viewing pleasure for you and your family for years to come.

Being an independent artist, I truly appreciate your business! I really want to personally <u>thank you</u>!

You should know that a recent painting I did was auctioned locally for more than $10,000.00! My work is featured at local art shows, and my original *Silent Tempest* painting has been on display in the Wadsworth Atheneum In Hartford since 1998. That means if you hold onto your painting, you'll likely see its value increase considerably.

As you may know, I also paint custom portraits, landscapes, abstract art, and theme-based artwork from your choice of subjects.

What does that mean for you?

Good question. I just moved into a new, more spacious studio, and I'm having a special sale just for my best customers. Here's what I want you to do (you'll love this): call me right away for a absolutely FREE, no obligation quote on any custom painting you'd like me to do for you. But…

Don't tell me you have this letter

until after I give you my free no-hassle quote.

Only then tell me that you have this letter, and I'll knock off an additional 21% off of my already ridiculously low price.

That way you'll know <u>for</u> <u>sure</u> I haven't "padded" my price just to give the appearance of a sale. I'm going to let you trick *me!*

Why would I do this? Simple. I want you as a customer for life. Most of my customers come back again and again, because they love my inspiration and extraordinary use of colors. And they appreciate the fact that <u>no other local artist</u> enjoys an appreciation on the value of *their* paintings as I do.

So call me today at (555) 555-5555 for your FREE quote.

Very Truly Yours,
John Artist

P.S. Remember, call me right away to take advantage of this most exclusive offer for my best customers <u>only</u>.

P.P.S. Also, don't tell me that you have this letter until *after* I give you my rock bottom price first!

Ok, obviously that's fictitious (it's a reprint from a sample letter I included in my Money Magnet newsletter). Plus I personally wouldn't use price as a selling point for an artist (unless your market warrants it), but you get the idea.

One car salesman collects the name and address of everyone who comes in to check out a car. Then he sends them a personalized letter, thanking them for stopping by, and telling more about the car they looked at, it's features, benefits, etc. Even if it results in one more sale a year (and he gets more than that), it's worth it in his case.

Event Marketing – Ever see those plaza store events, like when a new Harry Potter book is released? All the stores get together and celebrate the launch of the book in different ways. Obviously there's the bookstore release, but the local video and game rental store gets in the act. So does the family restaurant, ice-cream vendor, and arcade. Even the dry cleaning store can get involved and pump up their business, if they stick to a common theme. And this is all announced ahead of time (with appropriate press releases, etc.) so people coming down know what to expect. "Oh, great, we can get the book for little Sally, I can drop off my suit at the cleaners, my wife can go to the apparel store. What a great time this will be for the whole family!"

Start a Talk Show – If you have regular content to deliver that your target market wants, your own local talk show may be another avenue to cut through the clutter. Where I live there are plenty of local access stations that have these types of programs, and in most cases the community stations are free to air your programs. Think nobody watches them? Well, you're not going to beat out *American Idol*, and even infomercials will likely edge you out, but informal surveys I've conducted tell me that people are aware of these shows, and sometimes watch all or a part of one during late night channel surfing. There are even some regular "shows" that some of the locals rely on for information they can't easily get anywhere else. The key is to not do the same boring thing everyone else is doing.

In my local *Rare Reminder* newspaper, a local cable-access talk show host who DOES have people watching advertises for guests. If you can't start your own talk show, why not appear as a guest on one? You can get a DVD recording of it to use as a lead generation device. You can get great leads that way if your target market is watching.

Word of Mouth / Viral Marketing – The key here is create something that people will want to share. Yes, the "tell a friend" scripts are good online. The gift certificate idea mentioned previously is another. But surely there's something you can think of to really "wow" them. You want to make them say "Wait until Jane sees this!"

One of the keys to making this work (and any sort of lead generation device) is to know your customer's lifetime value. In other words, what does your average customer in this market (using the type of lead generation you are doing) bring me in profits over their entire lifetime? Let's say it's $25,000. And let's say your method of gathering leads converts 10% of leads into customers. Do you think it's wise to spend $100 per lead of that type in your efforts? Seems like a no-brainer to me.

Volunteer – Besides making you feel good about helping a worthy cause, it's a great way to network if you can volunteer where you come into contact with prospects (or people who have frequent contact with your prospects).

Unusual Places for Ads – I should say "unused places." Wherever a space is zoned for advertising and it's blank, there's an opportunity to get your message out. The side of a van. The side of a *dumpster.* Wherever.

Be an In-house Speaker – Besides getting great fees to appear and speak, you establish yourself as the expert. And like your free local mini-seminar, it's a great place to pitch your products and services.

In-house Presentations – JP Maroney talked about the stadium pitch on our call. I believe he was referring to a Chet Holmes article that talked about in-house presentations and closing the sale. I'm not going to say it better than Chet, so I'll refer you to that article so you can read it yourself. Great stuff!

http://www.chetholmes.com/articles/increasing_your_sales_ratio.htm

Dimensional Mail – Or "lumpy mail," as it's known is a great way to get your letter opened! They just can't resist the lumpy package. After it's opened, however, your sales letter should do its job. If you have a successful sales letter, adding a dimensional object to it will almost always bump response. A great place to get these types of lumpy mail objects is from Mitch Carson at http://www.impactproducts.net.

Another place to get "million dollar bills" and related promotional items is http://www.milliondollarsource.com

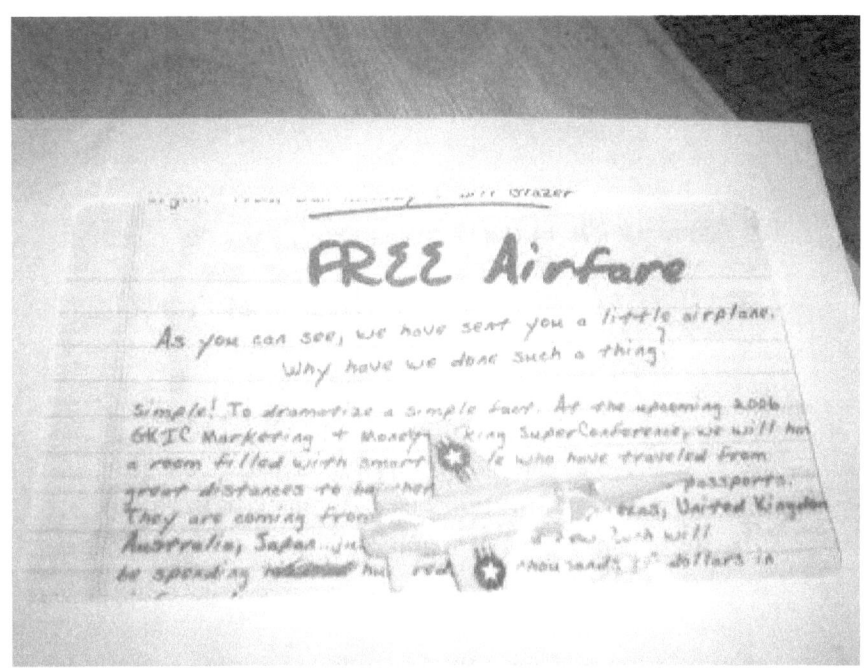

I received this dimensional mail package from Dan Kennedy. As you can see, the "lumpy object," a plastic airplane, was tied in with the offer, which included free airfare to one of Dan's seminars. Also note the "handwritten" letter. Stand out from the clutter!

Get Your Online List's Home Address and Phone Number – I spoke about this on the call. One technique Gary Halbert used was to ask his list for their home address, because he wanted to send them something to help them with their marketing. Then he sent them a lumpy mail package. But he got their home address. Now he can send them direct mail pieces and cut through all the email clutter by bypassing it completely (well, actually by supplementing it). Yanik Silver mentioned this as well. He obtains their home phone number and sends them a voice broadcast (see above). Joe Vitale does this too. So does Bill Glazer. Hmm, if all of these top marketers use this technique, do you think it works?

▤🖮① **Going Out of Business** – If a business with the same target market as yours is going to shut down soon, why not acquire their customer list? Most brick and mortar businesses consider liquidating their inventory or equipment, but not all of them are savvy enough to sell their customer list. That could be a huge opportunity for you.

▤🖰① **Alternate Franchise** – You know most franchises cost big bucks to buy into. Let's say you have a profitable cleaning business that's not a franchise, with your own system for success. You can teach this system to others and sell it for much cheaper than a franchise would go for. Here's an example of a company that does just that: http://www.my-mag-uk.com. I essentially do that with entrepreneurs. I teach them my marketing system (which as you probably know most entrepreneurs don't know a lot about effective marketing), and they gain a doubled or tripled profit margin as a result.

Or, you could locate such a successful company yourself, learn their system, and teach it to others in the same manner.

▤☙① **Office or Waiting Room Redesign** – If you have an office, waiting room, or reception area for your business, get rid of all magazines and replace them with testimonials and success story books, before and after photo albums, and other publications designed to advance the sale. Replace your wall paintings with framed testimonials. Give them an avalanche of proof!

▤▢① **Pre-paid Services** – Pre-paid "memberships" have been sold successfully by many businesses, such as cosmetic surgeons, chiropractors, dental services, martial arts schools, photographers, restaurants, you name it. The idea is to offer a bundle of services or products that would cost far more if purchased separately over time than if purchased pre-paid up front.

Reference USA – I mentioned this above in the "Direct Mail" topic, but it's worth its own topic. Why? Because if you have a library card, chances are you can access it for free. I don't pay the annual thousands of dollars required to access the site and compile lists of all sorts, because my local Newington library subscribes to it. My free library card gets me in for free. http://www.referenceusa.com

Creative Business Cards – Besides using both sides of your business cards and putting a compelling benefits-oriented message on it, there are many other creative ways to put your business card to work for you. Of course, odd-shaped and "rolodex-styled" cards stick out from the crowd as well. One real estate agent in California hands an extra three bucks and a business card to the toll collector as he crosses the bridge into San Francisco. He tells the toll collector that he wants to pay for the driver behind him, and asks him to give the driver his business card. Nine out of ten times, the driver calls, at least to say thank you. He's sold several expensive homes that way as a result.

A good lead generation device is to offer a free report or other gift on the back of the card. Then just distribute them where your prospects live.

At my local Munson's Chocolates outlet, Sales Manager Jim Florence has his business card fully imprinted with the company logo, name, phone number, and email address made out of…you guessed it…CHOCOLATE! (best business card I've ever eaten). A relatively new technology now allows Munson's to "print" in edible ink everything from text, images, logos, and photographs. With their business cards, customers get to *taste* their USP. How many other businesses offer that experience?

Ask Your Customers – It may sound super simple, but if you just ask your customers what they want and then give it to them, you'll be ahead of your competitors. For example, there's a local dentist who advertises on the radio that he offers a little pill that will put patients to sleep. While they snooze, he fixes years of neglect and damage in one visit. Without asking his customers, he may not have come up with this tremendous USP.

Do Research to Find Out What They Want – Again, this seems like a simplistic idea, but you'd be surprised how often it's overlooked. For instance, that same dentist I just mentioned above also advertises that nobody in his office will ever lecture you about avoiding visits to a dentist or failing to care properly for your teeth. They'll cheerfully do the work that you need and that you want, without guilt or hassle. That's a powerful benefit that most patients would probably not volunteer to tell their dentists, if asked. But by researching what dental patients complain about, and why they avoid going to the dentist as often as they should, he's addressed another powerful benefit of going to see him.

Positioning – Jay Conrad Levinson and Seth Godin talk about this in *The Guerrilla Marketing Handbook*. When Tom's of Maine introduced their "all natural" toothpaste, they didn't want to directly compete with all the other toothpastes out there. So they positioned themselves as a healthy all natural alternative. They sold it in health stores instead of supermarkets. Close-Up toothpaste used a similar tactic. Whereas most other toothpastes emphasized "no cavities" and were more family-oriented, Close-Up targeted single people and emphasized "whiteness."

An excellent book on positioning is *Positioning: The Battle for Your Mind*, by Trout & Reis.

Video Brochure – The same advantages a CD salesletter (above) has over a print salesletter are even greater with a video brochure. You can film your own infomercial and even if it never airs, you can distribute it on a DVD or videotape. Unlike infomercials, which have some strict guidelines, video brochures can contain practically any format. You can use the "news broadcast" format, which is restricted in infomercials. The best video brochures are those that look like television programs, since that's what people expect to see when they are watching it. Testimonials can now contain video of the person speaking. Before and after shots are great in this format as well.

Data-Based Marketing – Data-based marketing can be as simple as sending a greeting card or other "touch" communications with your customers and prospects. A florist specializing in nationwide delivery of fresh orchids uses data-based marketing quite effectively. If you order a bouquet for a friend's birthday or anniversary, they note the date and occasion in their computer. Eleven months later, you'll receive a call from them, reminding you of the occasion and asking you if you'd like to send another bouquet. Restaurants do this all the time with the birthday gift certificates. Other companies take it a step further and know when their customers will need a reorder of their product. They'll send a coupon or other discount to make another sale (for example, an oil change). Nowadays with all of the "rewards" and "shopper's club cards," supermarkets and chain stores not only capture everything you purchase and when, they can send you coupons and discounts for those products you regularly purchase. Amazon sends you emails about books similar to ones you have purchased when they re released and during other promotions.

You may want to consider starting your own "rewards" type program or something similar.

Secret Sales – You can send your customers a postcard that has a secret discount from 10% to whatever on everything they buy in one visit. The catch is they have to come into your store to find out the amount of the discount. The chance that they may have a 75% off coupon, for example, is often irresistible to the customer.

Add Extra Amenities - For physical locations, such as a car dealership, consider testing an in-house diner, barber, coffee shop, putting green, wireless internet, video arcade, playrooms for children, book stores, manicurists, climbing walls, mini-museum, ice-cream shop, etc. These can work well especially for those businesses where their customers have to wait. It may sound extravagant, but many businesses, especially those that cater to the affluent, have done this with resounding success. Why do you think McDonalds added playgrounds to most of their restaurants? Why do upscale bookstores have coffee cafés? The list goes on.

Newsletters – Newsletters are a great way to keep in touch with your customers, offer them special discounts and coupons, inform them of upcoming events (a wine store can tell their customers about an upcoming wine tasting event, for example), give them recipes, articles, advice, tips on making the most of your products/services, and much more. It's a great place to slip in case studies, success stories, testimonials, and pitches for other products and services.

Here are some tips for running a successful newsletter:

❖ Don't make it a straight sales pitch. You want it to be something your customers look forward to receiving.

Too much advertising can turn them off and equate it with junk mail. Include quality content on a variety of subjects, not all related to your business. Don't be boring.

❖ Keep it regular and consistent. Don't send it three times in one month and then wait 2 months before sending it out again. Quarterly is fine, but monthly is much better.

❖ If you have trouble coming up with regular content or don't have the time to commit to a newsletter, there are services that will do it for you. Dan Kennedy has such a service . You can also subscribe to a content service such as Pages (http://www.blogger.com), where they give you royalty-free articles, artwork, and much more every month.

❖ Proofread your newsletter. A spellchecker won't flag "four" when it should have been "fore." Tools like Microsoft Word also have grammar checkers. Check for factual accuracy and make sure dates, times, and places are all correct. Double-check coupon amounts and other numerical figures.

❖ Once you develop a layout that works, try to keep it consistent from issue to issue.

❖ Make it easy on the eyes to read. Avoid white type on black or colored backgrounds. Don't use dark blue type on a light-blue background. Use serif fonts for the body text. Don't make it look like too much work to read. Use white space liberally.

❖ Have a plan before you launch your newsletter. You want to have specific goals about what you want it to do for you. Should it be written in first-person from the owner? Or third person, like most newspaper articles? Do you want to have regular columns or features? Guest writers? Do your homework up front.

- ❖ Always include your contact information, perhaps even on each page.
- ❖ Feature your customers regularly. They like to see their names in print, and it's always far better to let them sell you than for you to sell yourself.

▣☐◑ **Novelty Items** – You can put your message on t-shirts, hats, coffee mugs, pens and pencils, mouse pads, you name it. The trick is to have a compelling image or slogan. For example, a logo or business name is boring. But a clever message or picture with a web address will get noticed more and used more.

▣▤◑ **Go to the "Edge"** – Seth Godin talks about this in his book *Free Prize Inside*. Basically, the premise is that while your competitors sell to the "middle," you find ways to sell to the edge. It sets you apart from your competition, but it's not necessarily your USP. For example, the first release of that book came packaged in a cereal box with the prominent "Free Prize Inside" displayed.

Some more examples:

- ❖ A massage salon moves their chairs outside in the summer.
- ❖ A security guard company offers its guards dressed as Beefeaters, Buckingham Palace guards, paramilitary camo-wearing high-security guards, Matrix-type outfits, or even attractive white-collar uniforms.
- ❖ A local pub built their own custom jukebox of twenty-six thousand songs in it by ripping their 1,798 CDs into a computer.
- ❖ A restaurant in Manhattan makes the average Joe's wait, but gives the VIPs an unlisted number to get to the front of the line. Strangely enough, this pleases both groups (the VIPs love to get right in, and the average

folk feel special by going to an exclusive restaurant where celebrities dine and the wait is longer due to its popularity).

- Mexico has plenty of all-in-one resorts, but only one caters to overweight people.
- NakedNews.com tells the TV-style news like everyone else, but they, well, wear less.
- The Four Sisters restaurant in Myanmar doesn't bother with a check. You pay what you think the meal is worth.
- Did you ever notice how supermarkets reward their worst customers? Shoppers with the least amount of items get their own special express lane, but the poor schmuck who's buying tons of groceries (and worth much more to the store as a customer) has to endure the longest line. What if a grocery store had a special line for their best customers, staffed with extra baggers and other mechanisms to speed the checkout process?
- Commerce Bank is open seven days a week. Do you think there are people who wouldn't mind having the option to bank on Sundays? And Liberty Bank offers free ATM usage. They'll even reimburse you for fees charged by other bank's ATMs.
- A church in New York City holds an annual barbecue for fundraising. People come from miles away because if they don't, they have to wait a whole year to come again. The local German club near my house holds their German Festival every two years for precisely the same reason.
- Enterprise Rent-A-Car doesn't focus on airport rentals. But when you need a rental car for a few days while your car is in the shop, they are the first ones you call. Plus, they pick you up!
- In the instant Internet buying world, a lawn care company realized that waiting weeks for a lawn care quote was too long. By using satellite photos and public

tax records, they're able to quote a cost for service *before* their prospects are even contacted. Now they drive down the street with a stack of Frisbees, each affixed with a sticker containing the property address and price quote, and toss each Frisbee onto the lawn.

Part III - Free Advertising With Publicity

Publicity is a great way to reach a lot of people with a limited budget. The key is to have a message that is newsworthy, which obviously changes all the time. Years ago it was enough to launch a new website. Nowadays that's too common. As I'm writing this, there's a 12-year old girl making news because of an experiment she conducted for her school's science fair: she had fast-food ice samples tested for bacteria and compared those test results with samples of toilet water from those same fast-food restaurants (about 30% of the ice samples had more bacteria in it than the toilet water).

Besides ordering your next soft drinks sans ice, this illustrates something profoundly important: news sells. You need something fresh. Something the public would want to know about.

So, that being said, let's explore some ways to get your free publicity.

- **Write a Regular Column** – Whether in a newspaper, magazine, ezine, or offline newsletter, a regular column is a great way to establish you as an expert in your field. You can also send reprints to your clients and prospects to add proof to your sales letters and promotional materials.

- **Write an Article** – Articles can be anything from a short essay on a topic to a feature article in a magazine, newspaper, ezine, newsletter, you name it. Again, article reprints help the selling job in adding proof to your persuasion.

- **Align With a Charity or Other Non-profit Organization** – This is a great way to get free publicity. Let's say you've created a course on starting a mail-order business on a shoestring budget. You can hold a free seminar with local low-income families and youths, give a presentation, and then give them all free copies of the course. Be sure to issue press releases with your local newspaper, radio and television stations, and community publications. Stories like these make great humanitarian interest pieces for these media outlets. Who knows? You could be the next guest on Oprah or the Today Show!

Issue a Press Release – An oldie, but goodie. The trick is to make sure your press release is a newsworthy event. For example, starting a new newsletter is not necessarily a newsworthy event (but it might in certain niche markets for smaller publications). Issuing a press release about a large donation you are giving, complete with relevant background story might be newsworthy. It all depends on your target audience and the publication(s). Editors pick up press releases if they think there is news for their readers. They do not care about you or your company. Your press release must be framed that way. "What's in it for me" is very relevant here.

Create a Newsworthy Event – Here's an idea that a local stereo and electronics store did that *would* qualify for a newsworthy press release:

- ❖ They arranged a "superstition obstacle course" on Friday the 13th in their parking lot, complete with ladders to walk under, a roaming black cat, mirrors to break, umbrellas to open indoors, etc.
- ❖ They called all the local radio stations and invited their morning personalities to come down and take the obstacle course challenge.

- ❖ One radio station took them up on their offer, and broadcast live from the event.
- ❖ The result was that tons of people came down to their store to watch and take part. And of course pick up some gear or supplies while they were there. And that, of course, not only provided a boost in sales for that day, it brought in new customers and generated lots of "word of mouth" advertising for them.

Any business can do something like this; I don't care if you're a conservative lawyer or accountant. The key is to find a theme and run with it. There's no reason why a jeweler or restaurant couldn't do something like that for Valentine's Day. Or a local Irish pub could do for St. Patrick's Day. Or any retail outlet for Christmas. The list goes on and on.

Attend Special Events – Watch your local news and constantly be on the lookout for events in your area where you can increase your visibility. As always, the best lead generation methods are those that introduce your products and services by way of something free (in exchange for their contact information, of course).

Take Time to Get to Know Your Local Editors and Publishers – It's a lot easier to pitch a press release or idea if you already know someone on the inside. Years ago I was in the middle of writing a book, and I started shopping for an agent, figuring it was easier to go that route than to approach the publishers directly. My wife managed insurance policies at the time for a Fortune 500 company, and one of her clients was the publishing firm Simon & Schuster. One day she happened to be talking to a prominent editor, and she mentioned my book. The editor told her to have me send it to his VP, at his request. Just like that I was no longer an unsolicited submitter. It was (and to my knowledge still is) Simon & Schuster's policy to not accept unsolicited manuscripts. That contact alone allowed me to bypass that barrier.

📷🗂️① **Write a Book** – With Print on Demand (POD) publishers, nowadays it's easy and cheap to type up and edit a book in your favorite word processor, upload it to a POD's server, and have the book available for shipping within weeks or less. Books are also a great way to position yourself as the expert. There's something almost magical that takes place when you send your clients an autographed copy of your latest book. In their eyes, you instantly gain credibility. Your status becomes elevated. They are more likely to want to do business with you.

There's little doubt that successful people want to surround themselves with other successful people. And a book shows them that you are successful. It gives you prestige. You are now an author. It's far easier to dismiss your self-claims in a salesletter than it is from a book. The fact that anyone can have a book printed is irrelevant (at least for now).

If you don't have the time or patience to write a book, you have several options:

❖ You can dictate the book and have it transcribed (elance. com and guru.com are good places to get a transcript done for you, but there are many other places online and offline to have them done as well).
❖ You can have someone ghostwrite the book for you. Be sure to check out their previous work, though!
❖ You can hold a teleseminar by yourself or with other experts and have it transcribed and edited into a book.
❖ You can get together with other experts in your field and each contribute a chapter or two for a book.

❖ You can interview other experts and compile it into a book.

❖ You can take books that are in the public domain, update it for today, and release it as a book (you may want to consider legal resources to make sure your choice is actually in the public domain…it's not always straightforward).

As you can see, it's fairly easy to have a book done in very little time and at very little cost. Just be sure the subject and material is relevant and fills a need. Ideally a book can also be used as a selling device for a back-end item or as a lead generation device.

Blogs, Podcasts, etc. – Yes, this is supposed to be about offline marketing methods, but in today's information age, I would be amiss if I didn't mention them.

Check out:

❖ http://www.blogger.com
❖ http://www.typepad.com
❖ http://www.moveabletype.com

…for starters. The offline part comes in when you advertise your blog in the offline world as well (which you should).

Part IV - Joint Ventures

Joint ventures (JVs) are one of the best ways to lure new leads and customers. By partnering with other businesses whose customers are part of your market, you have an additional profit center of incremental income. For example, an attorney can refer his clients to an accountant, and the accountant in turn refers clients to the attorney. It's a win/win situation, because many times a new business will need both an attorney and an accountant. Depending on which one they approach first (the lawyer or accountant), they'll be referred to the other.

JVs can go much further than this simple arrangement, however. They can be very complex, and there can be 3-way deals going on. In fact, JV brokers make their money by taking a slice of the profits between two or more different businesses, where he has brokered the deal and set up everything between them.

The key to making these deals work is to make sure that you let a prospective JV partner know from the start that:

- ❖ You've discovered an additional profit center for them that they are probably unaware of (offer projected profits, if possible).
- ❖ The additional profit center will not detract in any way from their current income stream.
- ❖ The additional profit center will not incur any additional costs or labor on their part to implement.
- ❖ The additional profit center will not incur any risk whatsoever on their part.
- ❖ You will perform all of the leg work to set it up.
- ❖ They can stop at any time for any reason.

There are so many potential JVs that are possible that there's no way to cover every conceivable one here. So instead I will give some examples. Some of them may be applicable to your business. Some may not. And, like the accountant and lawyer example I gave above, it's not feasible for me to cover every type of business. Therefore, you should look at each example and see how it may apply to your business. These examples are designed to get you thinking creatively. By no means is this an exhaustive list. It's designed to put you in the right mindset, where you will look at your business and others around you and see possibilities that you never noticed before.

A great course on JVs is the *JV Mastery Course*, by Jay Abraham and Marc Goldman. It may be out of print now, but if you can get a hold of it, I highly recommend it. If you have it, you may recognize some of these examples from the course (no need to reinvent the wheel here). Others are variations and some examples that I have personally done.

One Tip: If you try to set up a JV with a business, and they already have a deal in place with someone else, you can take that information to their competitor and say "Your biggest competitor is already doing this." And if your partner ever decides to stop the JV deal, you can go to their competitors and say the same thing (**Hint**: if you let them know you are going to do that, they may reconsider). Never feel that you have to partner with one specific business exclusively. Ideally you should have JV deals going on all over the place.

You can also do JVs between your business and another, or you can broker JVs between two different businesses and take a cut.

Now, onward…

> ⌛📄① **Sell an Idea** – A lawyer knew how to make a million dollars in a year with one person and three associates. Since many attorneys don't make that much, he codified his knowledge and had someone sell it. A realtor had a list three times better than anyone else, so she trained other realtors for a fee. A lumber mill knew how to kiln dry wood and get greater quality wood in less time with half

the energy cost, saving him millions of dollars. He taught his techniques to other lumber mills. If there's something remarkable about your business, or something you know how to do better than 99% of everyone else, you have an opportunity to license or teach your skills to others.

⌛▤➀ **JV With Your Suppliers** – Your suppliers generally want you to be more successful, since it means more sales for them. They may fund sales people, mailings, extra staff, etc. You'll never know unless you ask them.

⌛▤➀ **Seek Out Other Business That Cater to Your Market** – I used the lawyer and accountant example above. A realtor may JV with moving companies, custom framers, carpet cleaners, pest control services, lawn care companies, painters, electricians, plumbers, the list goes on. Just be sure to JV with those businesses who have products and/or services your customers may need (i.e. a realtor JVing with a video game company doesn't make much sense).

Make a list of businesses who want and need a constant flow of leads: lawyers, doctors, dentists, realtors, home remodeling services, carpet cleaners, pest control services, etc. Broker deals between them where there is a fit to generate leads.

⌛▤➀ **Leverage Buyers and Sellers** – A business broker sent a letter to 30,000 CPA firms saying "We've got buyers ready to pay all cash to buy your practice whether you stay or not." 500 people responded, so he took those 500 people out and mailed the other 29,500 firms saying "We've got 500 hundred firms right now that are big money makers ready to be sold. Owners will stay or not. Terms or cash is your choice." Then it was a simple matter to match the buyers to the sellers, resulting in a million dollars worth of commissions. This is a very powerful technique that can be used in a variety of different ways.

⧗⧗◑ **Match Front-End/Back-End Products** – If you sell a high-ticket back-end product, you can seek out people who don't yet have a back-end product and JV yours via an affiliate program. Likewise, if you don't have a high-ticket back-end product, the reverse is also true. There are plenty of expensive product and service sellers out there to partner with.

You can also broker deals between businesses selling front-end books and tapes and businesses selling back-end expensive seminars, for example.

⧗▦◑ **JV a Sales Force** – There are plenty of professional sales people that sell a variety of different products on a commission basis. It's a snap to put an ad in the paper to get these folks to sell your products and services.

⧗✍◑ **The Neon Sign Approach** – I call this the "Neon Sign Approach" because Jay Abraham talked about a particular JV deal with a neon sign maker. He would have high school and college students drive around at night and look for neon signs that were not lit or only partially lit. Then he would pay them per "find," and report those locations to the neon sign maker. Voila! Instant leads.

A variation on this approach could be done with motor vehicles. There are numerous services to get the names and addresses from a motor vehicle registration plate. Those same high school and college students can be on the lookout for broken taillights, body damage, cracked windshields and the like. When they find one, they write down the license plate information and give it to you. You can then supply the leads to auto repair shops, body shops, windshield replacement shops.

What if you owned a furniture store? You could JV with door-to-door salespeople and have them on the lookout for badly worn furniture. They're already going to be in their prospect's living room, right?

How about the furnace maintenance person who keeps an eye out for water damage in the basement? If you offered basement-sealing services, wouldn't you want as many furnace maintenance folks as possible getting you leads?

⌛☎① **JV Mailings** – For certain product or service offerings, direct mail can be prohibitively expensive. That's why card decks and Value-Paks are so popular. But aside from those types of mailings, you can always partner with a non-competitor (or two or three) that offer a complementary or similar product/service with the same target market as yours. By splitting the cost of the mailing, you still get your message out, but at a much-reduced cost.

⌨▢① **JV Inserts/Flyers/Circulars** – Similar to JV mailings, you could arrange to have your flyer, insert, or circular inserted into another publication already being mailed. This "hitching a ride" approach works best when your audience is targeted, although newspaper inserts are popular with local bricks and mortar businesses. The JV part comes into play when you pay so much per lead or a percentage of all sales resulting from the arrangement. Depending on your price structure, you can pay a percentage of the first sale only, or a tiered approach where a smaller percentage is paid for all first year purchases, a percentage of the back-end purchase, etc. You need to determine what types of deals bring in the biggest profits for you, while still providing a valuable incentive for your JV partners. *And that really goes for any type of deal.*

📠🗁① **JV a Mini-Seminar or Teleseminar** – Using the lawyer/ accountant example again, the two could get together and hold a seminar for new business owners, offering a package deal for both of their services.

📠📄① **Sell Your JV** – When you have an income stream from a JV deal you have worked out, you can always sell the rights to that deal to someone else. Just like a money-making website that you can sell, JVs that have a positive cash flow are assets in their own right.

📠📄① **JV Deals to Observe and Learn From a Guru** – Basically, you can act as a broker or middle agent between a person with a certain expertise and others who want to learn from the expert.

📠📄① **If You're the Guru, Vice Versa** – If you are the expert, the reverse is also true. You could JV with a middleman to bring people to you to pay for access to your expertise. Coaching programs are an obvious choice for this approach.

📠📄① **JV a Dealmaker** – If brokering deals isn't your forte, you can always JV with someone who sells well and knows how to negotiate to pitch and put the actual deals together for you. This way you can sit back and pull all the strings while your "agent" handles the stuff you aren't comfortable doing.

📠⏳① **Painting Fire Hydrants** – One of the first deals Jay Abraham put together was paying kids to paint fire hydrants. He'd put all the deals together, the kids would go out and paint, and he'd pay them a percentage of what he was getting paid. His value was that he was the one to put it all together, he set up the deals, and he got the labor organized. This approach works well anytime there is someone willing to perform the service for less that you are getting paid.

Even 'ol Tom Sawyer did this when he had to white wash a fence in Mark Twain's *Tom Sawyer*. He got the local kids to do it, and they loved it.

⌨⌨① **Overstock/Surplus Selling** – It's not difficult to find businesses with excess inventory, tie up the rights to unload it at a discount, then find outlets to sell it at retail. You pocket the difference. On the flip side, if you yourself have excess inventory, you could JV to find someone to unload it from you in the same fashion.

⌨☝① **JV to the Affluent** – If you can partner with a business that sells a high-ticket item to the affluent, here's a blueprint worth testing:

❖ Choose the most popular high-ticket item they sell.
❖ Send a letter via Fedex to their "A" list, those 20% of customers that are responsible for 80% of their profits. Tell them about a special one-day closed door private by invite-only "showing" for that one specific product/ service. Hire a professional copywriter to write a specific sales letter for that one product or service.
❖ Serve coffee, tea, muffins, or whatever is appropriate for that target market on the day of the showing. Make it an event, more than just the product or service itself. Look for ways to gain media exposure. Yes, it's a private showing, but if their "A' list hears about it from the media, they'll want to be there.
❖ Make sure they have their most knowledgeable staff on hand for the showing. You're selling to the affluent here, so you don't want to cut any corners. Find out what they want and give it, to them.
❖ Collect your profits, but be sure to follow-up with a thank you letter, ideally also Fedex'd to them. And unadvertised bonuses always help!

Lead Generation JVs – Find out what other businesses your target market visits. For example, I sell to entrepreneurs, and a lot of them frequent the UPS Store and other such places. Fedex/Kinkos and other "copy shops" are also ideal places where I live. Many of these places don't capture their customer's name, address, email address, etc. So I made an arrangement with them. I setup "take ones," where they can take a brochure for free, go online to my website, fax me, or mail me their contact info, then I send them a free report relevant to them. I give their contact info to the store I JV with (and I notify the prospects of this fact… it hasn't seem to hurt my leads significantly so far). For those businesses (a Staples store, being one of them) that are stubborn, I offer to give them the contact info I collect from all the stores I JV with in their area. Again, you need to include a disclaimer when doing that, but in my tests, the benefit has outweighed the losses.

In a discussion with Michel Fortin recently, he mentioned that you need to really provide an incentive for these businesses to promote you. So the "take one" box may not be enough by itself. True, they are getting the contact info of some of their customers (something they themselves should be gathering), but if they don't know enough to get that information in the first place, they may not be as anxious to promote your free report or premium. I'm experimenting with several other ways to measure how well they will promote me, and I'll provide updates as they become available.

Endorsements – There are people and businesses that have a great personal relationship with their customers and prospects. They may not necessarily know this fact. In fact, a lot of them don't even realize the amount of pull they have with their audience. People who recommend certain stocks or trends, people who give great content and information to their subscribers, people who give investment advice, generally people who have a certain rapport with their subscribers. They are the ones you want to target. If their niche is non-marketing-related, so much the better in order to cut through this niche's clutter. I know someone who targeted golf enthusiasts for a marketing product, simply because of their test results. In any case, if you can JV with this sort of person who will endorse your product or service, you have a huge advantage. It's simply one of the best ways to print money on demand. Please don't overlook this technique.

These people may not even realize the relationship they have with their list. So you would be well advised to start with those folks.

JV Your List Building: Large List – If you have a large list, one of the easiest ways to build it even further is to do a cross mailing. That is, you partner with another large list owner in your target market. You send out his message to your list, he sends out your message to his list. Simple. Just remember, once your prospects or customers are on another list that sells to them, there is increased message clutter. That is, they are now being pitched by your JV partner AND you. It's a tradeoff you need to consider.

JV Your List-Building: Small List – Ok, if your existing list isn't large enough to warrant a cross JV mailing as described above, here's a clever way to build your list up quickly. I've done this, but not to the extent I should. I've got more deals like this in the works. Here's how it works:

Let's say your list is on the small side. "John Smith" has a huge list. You want to JV with him, but a cross swap isn't going to persuade him. You need to be the middleperson between John Smith and another large list owner.

"Jane Doe" is another huge list owner. What if you can put John Smith and Jane Doe together to do a cross mailing, and you get exposure as well. Instead of a cut of profits, you agree to get a slice of the list. In other words, perhaps in order to get onto Jane's list from John's, they have to come through you first. Or, you could have John mail his list with the agreement that whatever prospects Jane gets, she'll share with you. It's a win/win/win situation, because all of you are gaining new prospects on your lists.

John gets some of Jane's list.

Jane gets some of John's list.

You get some of Jane's list. Or, ideally, you get some of both lists. You are the dealmaker. It wouldn't have happened without you, so depending on the deal you make, why shouldn't you get access to both lists?

⌐▤◑ **JV Advertising Space** – Remnant advertising is big business these days for those who how to exploit it. What is remnant advertising, aka "stand-by advertising?" A reprint from my newsletter will explain:

If you already have an effective direct mail campaign, why not tweak the same winning letter and turn it into a space ad? You already have a winning piece. You can save on costs by merely reformatting it a little to create a whole new ad. Of course, depending on your sales letter, this may or may not work. Some letters are specifically targeted for a particular niche market (as they should be). In that case, you may need to change the headline or tweak the lead, but it can usually be done for a lot less than writing a new ad from scratch. And you also gain the added advantage of speed. You can get your space ad written in this fashion a lot *faster* than writing from scratch. Of course, that's assuming you have the budget to take out half-page or full-page ads. What if your budget only allows for a smaller space ad?

One of the most challenging things about small space ads is trying to fit in enough copy to get the job done. "The more you tell, the more you sell" is especially true when the goal of the ad is to provoke an action from the prospect, especially an action that involves more than just picking up the phone or dropping a reply card in the mail.

So what's the most effective type of space you can use in a newspaper, publication or even on the web?

A larger one. One that gives you plenty of room to include your long and persuasive copy. If a prospect doesn't know enough about your product or service, and isn't convinced enough to act immediately, you've lost an opportunity. Repeat this to a circulation of tens or hundreds of thousands, and your ad is like flushing perfectly good money right down the toilet.

So this advertising concept; Stand-by Advertising is worthy of Further Exploration as I have used the concept many, many times succesfully and I will explain it further on this promotional sample letter written by me.

Dear Advertising Director,

Over the past several years, many clients have expressed an interest in having their advertisements published in your newspaper,(or magazine,wesite etc.)

However, after comparing your open rate with that of other publications where the advertisement has already been published we have no option but

to advise the client not to use your publication,(newspaper,magazine, website etc.) due to the fact that our clients advertisements have been only profitable in Those publications where a stand-by or remnant rate has been offered.

As you know, the use of space is very important to any advertiser or publication. Stand-by simply means a newspaper agrees to publish an advertisement whenever or wherever space becomes available and offers to reduce the open line rate to the advertiser for "standing by". It often happens that "Empty" space may become available due to last minute cancellations of scheduled advertisements or because of production difficulties. Many times this "new" available space is filled with house ads or public service ads to fill the hole or space and the publications receive no revenue for this space.

That is why stand-by advertising is becoming very advantageous for <u>both</u> the publications and the advertiser. The newspaper (or magazines, websites etc.) can make money on space it might otherwise have to give away. The advertiser is able to use a publication or website it could not use at the open rate.

More and more publications are becoming involved in stand-by advertising. Have your publication offered a stand-by rate in the past or present? If not we would like very much for you to consider this possibility now. We are open to do business with you by exploring the possibility of sending you an insertion order for a full page ad, a mechanical and a check for the new amount of the order. The net amount would be computed at the open rate discounted by 50% for stand-by, normal for the industry, and 15% for the standard agency discount. Then when "empty" Space become available you can use the check and send us a tear sheet.

Please let us know if this is something that you would be interested in doing. Remember that Publication space is all too valuble and that you can increase your advertising revenue if you accept our offer.

Please feel free to call me if you have any questions. My phone number is: XXX-XXX-XXXX. My email is: JuanMarcial@ProfitPotentials.net

Sincerely,
Juan Marcial

The newspaper or publication just can't resist the fact that they might have a check in hand, more profits for them, for utilizing advertising space that would have otherwise yielded zero dollars in revenue.

In doing some reseach on this matter, It has been reported that advertisers typically pay 3 times the amount for a

4-inch by 4-inch ad than they can get for a quarter-page ad. Some of them can even get ads at around **10% the normal going rate**! And that includes agency fees. That means with stand-by advertising, you can get the same size ad as your competitors for one-tenth the cost!

I suggest you check out the following about this concept and its originator from the Gary Halbert Letter at:

http://www.thegaryhalbertletter.com/newsletters/zkkj advertising more profitable.htm

It includes another sample letter plus a lot of useful information from Gary. I won't repeat what Gary said about positioning your ad, or any of the great advice he gave, so head on over to read it all.

By the way, if you haven't heard of Gary, he was one of the best marketers and copywriters in the world. He is now dead but his advise and genius will always be with us. I highly recommend reading all his newsletters and materials if you don't already which you can find at:

http://www.thegaryhalbertletter.com

There are more proven marketing ideas in his newsletters than there are leaves on a tree, so get on over there and start reading. WARNING: If you're like me, you'll have trouble sleeping after reading it, because your mind will be racing with ideas!

So how can this benefit a JV enthusiast? Well, what do think some Ad Agencies like us are doing? We are doing deals with publications around the country and offering reduced advertising costs to our clients. If you're a marketing consultant, do you think we can help you and your clients? Is it possible to make your own deals with newspapers, magazines, and other publications? You betcha! Jay Conrad Levinson even talks a great deal about this in his Guerilla Marketing books. You merely need to move beyond concept into ACTION!

✒📄① **Rekindle Procrastinating Customers** – Here's something you can do for your own business, or you can do a JV with another business and capture some of the "found" revenue. Many customers tend to procrastinate on their purchases. For example, a dentist may have 3000 patients, but after analysis, 1000 haven't come back in over a year. A sequence of mailings to these 1000 (with incentives to come back) might bring back a certain percentage, of which you can negotiate up front a slice of the profits.

This may be nothing new to you. But most dentists know about dentistry, not marketing.

Or how about the carpet salesman who has customers that haven't replaced their carpets in six years. If the average customer replaces his carpet every five years, you have an opportunity to offer them an incentive to act now.

✒📄① **Rekindle Former Customers** – In addition to customers that procrastinate, there will always be customers, for one reason or another, that no longer purchase from a business. Perhaps they've moved out of the area. They may no longer have a need for your product/service (i.e. baby clothes…the baby eventually grows up). They may have passed away. There are lots of reasons why. And then there are those customers who are dissatisfied.

You want to target most of them. For those that are dissatisfied, you want to offer them an opportunity to make things right, to give them a special deal if they agree to give you another try.

For the others, they are most likely satisfied former customers. For whatever reason, though, they are no longer part of the target market. The best way to capitalize on that situation is to get them to refer business to you. If they are satisfied, they may respond favorably to a gift certificate that they can pass onto a friend or relative who IS still part of the target market.

Either way, it's "found" business, and you stand to profit from it.

Let's say you want to target chiropractors. You can locate a bunch of authors who are reputable and recognized by chiropractors, contact them, and tell them what you're doing. Ask to buy a bunch of copies of their book at a discount if they would be willing to send a letter to these chiropractors along with their book (at your expense). The letter would say something like, "Hi, this is John Smith here. You probably know me through my book, '17 Ways to Grow Your Chiropractor Business Today.' It's been reviewed in *Health Economics*, and I'm sending you a copy of my book with my compliments and introducing you to Jane Doe, because she's got a great way to reactivate your no longer active patients. I've asked her to email you in about a week."

✏️💡 **JV With an Agent to Bring in "Found" Business** – If you want to focus on your core business, like the dentist example I mentioned about (i.e. let's say that you're the dentist), and you're not sure how to go about bringing in this "found" business, there are experienced marketers out there who could handle the nuts and bolts of the campaign. In other words, this would be the reverse of the previous two examples, where you are the professional, and a deal with a marketer would yield you additional business, but without the marketing headaches. At the very least you could pay someone to teach you how its done, or learn by example in observing their methods and asking questions.

⌐🖲① **JV a Consulting Back-End With a Static Product Seller** – Let's say that you are a consultant specializing in doing creative real estate deals. You could find someone who sells a static book or course on the subject, then partner with them to offer your coaching or consulting services on the back-end for those that want to go beyond the book or course. You could offer your own course, seminars, coaching programs, whatever.

⌐⌐① **JV a Static Product With a Consulting Back-End** – And the opposite is also true. If you sell a static information product, why not seek out an expert on the subject that you can partner with and endorse for additional training for your customers. Everybody wins!

⌐🝙① **Tie Up the Rights to Real Estate** – I don't mean real estate in the traditional sense. I mean space. Using the chiropractor example, what if you opened a satellite office that's manned once or twice a week in a health club or health food store? You could put lots of things in those places. Acupuncture, Shiatsu, massage therapy, weight-loss clinics, exercise products, the list goes on.

Instead of an office, you could tie up the rights to a display space or an impulse buy counter near the register. How about a segment of the store, the rear section of a store, or the front corner where merchandise or services can be placed? Banks now put branches in grocery stores. So do flower shops. Sears put Allstate Insurance in their stores and created a billion dollar business. Designer shampoos have space in salons.

If you tie up the space first, then you can go out and find inventory that you will in essence consign to the space. Anywhere there is foot traffic is really fair game. Just be sure to find a product or service that is a match to the foot traffic's preferences (i.e. the target market).

There are lots of one or two-person companies who manufacture their own jewelry, or candy, or cookies, or toys, or crafts. Maybe a local hotdog joint doesn't have cookies on their menu. Put them together and take a cut. How about craft supplies and raw materials at a craft show? A service in a hotel that perhaps that hotel doesn't offer? Maybe free wireless Internet access in exchange for their contact info. The nice thing is you don't have to put up any inventory.

Vacant lots are great to put in cars for sale. Or organize your own flea market or craft show. A haunted house around Halloween, sponsored by the local costume shop. A golfing goods tent that coincides with the timing of the US Open.

I've mentioned some of these ideas already, but this example is about tying up the rights to space. Get the rights first, then looks for ways to fill it.

📷🗔🌓 **JV With Those Who Already Have Business Relationships** – I mentioned at the start of this section that some of the best companies to JV with are those whom you already have a preexisting relationship with. What if you don't have any?

You can JV with those people who do! Put an ad in your local paper. Go online and network with people who do have these relationships. Then cut them in on the deal and let them introduce you. <u>It's the difference between a cold intro and a warm or hot one</u>.

Start Small – Do you have a big idea for a deal but no relationship with the potential partner company? You can always start out small, with a test to validate your experience and the results before moving onto the big deal you had in mind. By the time your small deal is validated, you know have that relationship to move to the next level.

Let Them White Label You – Let's assume you are an IT consulting firm, and you decide to JV with hardware companies to access their customer base and have them endorse your services. The trouble is, you want to JV with several hardware makers, and each one wants you to use only their hardware. How do you get around that and still have access to all of their lists and endorsements?

One way is to let them "white label" your services. In other words, when you consult for their customers, you represent that hardware company. So every time you go out, you change "shirts and hats," so to speak. That way each hardware company has you representing them. Basically, they would sell your services as their own.

Think of it as a "private label rights" situation, where you sell your works to other companies that they can in turn repackage as their own. If you're looking to drum up more business, this one approach alone could bring you more than you can handle. In other words, you may have to hire more staff. It's <u>that</u> powerful.

Listen, do you think all of the "Geek Squads" and such are all owned by the companies dispatching them? No, many are contracted. These are large-scale corporate deals, but nothing says you can't do something similar on a smaller scale to start.

◌▤◑ **JV the Costs** – Whether it's an office you share, or a receptionist, or an administrative assistant, or standby conference call lines, you can make deals with other businesses that may not need a full-time receptionist, for example, to keep the costs down. A local school supply business shares an office with a surveyor. A small downtown Hartford mail order firm shares office space and conference rooms with an advertising agency. A New York investment consulting firm shares the mailing address with a Florida realtor who is also licensed in New York and wants a local presence. Things like office and mail services, help desk support, and other shared services are becoming more common. If you can't find one that makes sense for your business, why not invent your own solution?

◌▤◑ **JV to Build Your List** – Your list is your greatest asset, right? But if you only have 1,000 names where 50,000 or 100,000 is the norm (more is better, right?), then why not JV a list exchange. Bear with me. It's true that you may not have much to offer to the list owner of 100,000+ names, when you only have 1,000. But it can be done.

One way to do this? Ok, let's pretend that I convince a speaker to do a teleseminar with me that I know at least 2 or 3 other 100k+ list size owners would love to tell their subscribers about. Let's couple that with the fact that these list owners want to build their lists even more. And you do too. You could make a deal with some of these list owners that whoever opts in to your teleseminar, you'll do a solo mailing of a product of their choice to the entire list if they promote the call. Remember they're delivering a message to their list that their list would be interested in, and they're interested in getting the names of the other list owners that will opt-in. So you act as the middle-person and make all sides happy, while greatly adding to the size of your list.

I've personally done this, and I've got some big promotions on the way that will grow my list even further. All you need to do is to contact these people and let them know how they benefit from the arrangement.

Will everyone welcome the deal? No. But there are plenty who will. And everyone wins (those are the best kinds of deals, by the way). This is one of those ideas that will work just as good online as they do offline.

ⅧⅨ **School Deals** – You can contact local community colleges and other educational learning institutes and offer to teach a course for free or for a salary. While you'll teach them valuable skills, the logical outcome of your course is for them to purchase your full-course and other information products. While I haven't personally done this, I know of others who have, and it's a great way to both establish you as an expert and make money on the back-end as well. And the inevitable publicity doesn't hurt, either.

ⅧⅨ **Company Speeches/Seminars** – Lots of companies give in-house speeches and seminars. Most charge a nominal sum. You can do the same, and sell your products and services. It's a great way to get into a company and do your pitch.

ⅧⅨ **Friends and Relatives** – One of the best ways to get started in JV deal making is by working with people you already know well and who trust you. I'm talking about friends and relatives who are entrepreneurs. Look, there's a reason why MLM companies like Tupperware and the Pampered Chef do so well. Most of their first-time salespeople sell to their friends and relatives first.

My younger brother sold a set of knives to my mother that she still uses to this day (after years). I used to sell Mason Shoes door to door when I was a teenager (yes, admittedly a LONG time ago). Guess who my first buyers were?

Well, the same thing works for JVs. I have some friends who opened up a restaurant. I'm now working with them, without any money out of their pocket, to develop JV deals that will build additional profit centers for them. And yes, I get a cut.

When you work with folks that are close to you, you tend to have their vested interest at heart. And that sets the stage for JV deals with "cold" prospects, because you also want to be known as having their best interests at heart.

You are the dealmaker. You make it happen and know all of the ins and outs of business. This comes with time, so the more deals you make (even the unprofitable ones), the better you'll be equipped to handle the bigger more profitable ones.

JV Anything You Need – Need a room to hold your seminar? A rental car? Your hotel or airfare covered? Any expense, rental, or use of a product or service? Why not use your product or service to JV what you need. Michel Fortin used to do this with a local hotel. He would get the room for free and hold all of his seminars there, getting new leads and business. While his seminar attendees were there, they used the hotel's business center, giving the hotel business as well. It was a win/win situation.

JP Maroney worked out a deal to get his room for free to hold his mini-seminar as well. Jay Abraham regularly did deals to get cars, airfare, you name it.

ଘଘ ① **JV for Airtime** – Yes, it's even possible to JV with radio and television stations for free airtime for your ads and infomercials. Every radio or television station has some unsold airtime. They have to use it for something. They only need to fill a certain amount of public service time. After that, the rest of the time is used for the most profitable way they can come up with. If you present a compelling offer to them, yours may be more desirable to them. Simply find out what they want, and offer it to them for an exchange of airtime.

NOTE: This technique is done more often than you think, mostly by ad agencies and bigger companies. But even with that going against you, there is still a considerable amount of unsold time available, especially in the smaller stations. **Hint:** You *don't* have to do the deal with only one station at a time.

$$$ **Leverage JV with Bartering** – This is another little-known technique you can use to make your deals even more lucrative.

Let's say that you found out that your local radio station WXXX needs a new roof. So you do a deal with the local roofing company J&J Roofing, where you trade your services for a roofing job. J&J charges $10,000 for a new roof needed by WXXX. But it only costs them $3,000 in labor and materials. The other $7,000 is profit. So you provide $3,000 worth of services to J&J, get $3,000 worth of labor and materials in result, and are able to give WXXX a new $10,000 roof for only $3,000 worth of services. Now *you* get J&J's $7,000 profit.

Listen, it does work that way more often than you think. Jewelry, cars, furniture, services, and just about anything you can think of produced by a for-profit company always has that kind of leverage if you work the deal the right way.

$$$ **"Think Outside the Box"** – Yes, I know it's a cliché.

But in this case, it's very true and profitable. The examples I provided here aren't by a long shot every possible technique you can use. Rather, they are designed to get you thinking in the proper "mindset." You'll soon see that there are more possibilities and opportunities around you that you may have not noticed before. So your job is to always be on the lookout for them. And recognize them when they do catch your attention.

Will they always be profitable? Hardly. But as you get more and more exposed to this kind of creative marketing thinking, you'll be better equipped to spot the ones that *are* more frequently up front.

The best advice I can give you to that end is to try some of these ideas for yourself. Make them your own. Find out what works best for your business and which ones don't. Read more than one newspaper each day. Read trade journals and magazines. Read what your target market reads. There's opportunity everywhere if you know where to look.

Conclusion

I hope these examples have helped you to develop the mindset to be on the lookout for **opportunities everywhere**.

I've tried to arrange these ideas in a logical format, so you can assess them out and go through each one with a highlighter and pen, making notes, and adding your own thoughts.

There's a great quote: "**More occurs from movement than will ever happen from meditation and contemplation**." And so I would strongly urge you to take action. Don't just read this and put it on a shelf or bury it on your computer's hard drive. Read it. Use it. Own it.

Take action and reap the rewards. To your great success!

Part V - Before You Do Any Business

If you really want to make real money and reach all the Happiness, and Real Sucess in your life, pay very close attention to this part of the book because it is short but it is **The Most Important Part.**

Success come to all those who serve others and help others in life. Don't be in business just for the money, be in business because you sincerely want to help others to get to their goals.

There is a Compensation Law in nature that most people ignore and that will bring back to you all the blessings and all the Good that you bring to the rest of humanity in a personal and a collective way.

This Law is responsible also for all our problems and failures when we fail to take it into account and act selfishly and do harm to others even unconsciously or because of our ignorance.

And talking about ignorance Never, ever, ever, stop learning new things to improve yourself and your business. You never know when a Million Dollar idea will come to your mind thru reading, listening to a program or even on a seminar you attend.

So invest in yourself and your learning and also listen to your inner voice that is the True Source of all Great Ideas in the Universe. Be Good my friend and be Truly Happy !!!

I wish You The Best
Juan Marcial (The King Of Marketing And Promotions)

Resources

For More Information, Resources And Updates,
Visit our Web Page At:

http://www.profitpotentials.net/book

Here you will find a FREE Bonus Chapter based on a Secret Report on the subject of Creativity and Mental Creation in Marketing. This information is so CONFIDENTIAL that it cannot be published in book form in any way and we only share it with the Readers of this Book.This information will really help you Wake Up The Marketing Genius Inside of You !!!

And again this is All FREE Only to the Readers of this Book !!!